YOUNG GUNS

Every year a new crop of talented youngsters burst onto the scene, making their first steps on the road to becoming footballing superstars.

To celebrate the best starlets around, we take a look at a cluster who have what it takes to make it all the way to the top.

JACK GREALISH +

DOB: SEPTEMBER 10, 1995

After signing a new four-year deal at Aston Villa in October 2014, the attacking midfielder has already impressed many with his dazzling displays, most notably with two assists in the club's 2015 FA Cup semi-final win over Liverpool.

RUBEN LOFTUS-CHEEK +

DOB: JANUARY 23, 1996

The tall central midfielder made his debut for Chelsea as a substitute in the Champions League against Sporting Lisbon in December 2014 and was promoted to the first-team squad by Jose Mourinho in February 2015.

JORDON IBE +

DOB: DECEMBER 8, 1995

After impressing during a loan spell at Championship side, Derby County, the winger was recalled to Anfield in January 2015 and produced a number of eye-catching performances with his direct, attacking style.

MARTIN ODEGAARD +

DOB: DECEMBER 17, 1998

After appearing for Norway at the age of 15, the attacking midfielder then moved to Real Madrid, where he made his first-team debut aged 16. A mercurial talent with a big future.

PIERRE-EMILE HOJBJERG +

DOB: AUGUST 5, 1995

The midfielder became the youngest player to appear for the Bayern Munich first-team when he came on in April 2013 at the age of 17, and he has already made a number of appearances for the Danish senior side.

DELE ALLI +

DOB: APRIL 11, 1996

The young midfielder made his name with MK Dons, and joined Tottenham in February 2015 for a fee of £5m. He was loaned back to the Dons named as the You and named Player of the Year at the 2014-15 Football League Awards.

The voice of football

SHOOT

Published 2015.
Pedigree Books Limited, Beech Hill House,
Walnut Gardens, Exeter, Devon EX4 4DH
www.pedigreebooks.com
shoot@pedigreegroup.co.uk

EDITOR
DANIEL TYLER

ASSISTANT EDITOR
JAMES BEAVIS

DESIGN
JONATHAN FINCH

WWW.SHOOT.CO.UK

@SHOOTMAGAZINE

CONTENTS

RUBEN NEVES

DOB: MARCH 13, 1997

The midfielder is already a regular in Porto's team after making his league debut, and scoring, at the age of 17. He made his bow in the Champions League five days later and is known for his accurate passing.

JOE GOMEZ

DOB: MAY 23, 1997

After coming through Charlton Athletic's youth system, the tall centre-back, who can also play right-back, became a regular in the Championship side's defence in the 2014-15 season. He also helped England win the 2014 European Under-17 Championship and has since earned a £3.5m move to Liverpool.

YOURI TIELEMANS

DOB: MAY 7, 1997

Considered to be one of the brightest young talents in world football, the midfielder made his debut for Anderlecht at the age of 16 in the Champions League in October 2013, and scored eight goals in 51 appearances in 2014-15.

BREEL EMBOLO

DOB: FEBRUARY 14, 1997

The Cameroon-born Swiss forward enjoyed a breakthrough season with FC Basel in 2014-15, scoring 17 goals and picking up 13 assists in 42 appearances, as well as making his debut for Switzerland's senior side.

DEMARAI GRAY

DOB: JUNE 28, 1996

The young winger broke onto the scene for Birmingham City in the 2014-15 Championship season, in which he scored a hat-trick against Reading. With pace, good dribbling and technique, an exciting future awaits.

ALEKSANDAR MITROVIC

DOB: SEPTEMBER 16, 1994

Already a full Serbia international, the tall striker made a huge impact with Belgian side Anderlecht following a move from Partizan Belgrade in 2013, scoring 28 goals in 51 appearances in the 2014-15 season. This resulted in a big money move to Newcastle United in the summer of 2015.

KIT SWAP

CHECK YOUR ANSWERS ON PAGE 61

OH NO! THE KIT MAN'S HAD A SHOCKER AND MIXED UP THESE FOUR STARS' INTERNATIONAL STRIPS. CAN YOU WORK OUT WHICH SHIRT, SHORTS AND SOCKS BELONG TO WHICH PLAYER?

GARY CAHILL **LIONEL MESSI** **MESUT OZIL** **DIEGO COSTA**

A — 10

B — 19

C — 5

D — 8

A — 8

B — 5

C — 19

D

A

B

C

D

SHIRT ☐ SHORTS ☐ SOCKS ☐

SHIRT ☐ SHORTS ☐ SOCKS ☐

SHIRT ☐ SHORTS ☐ SOCKS ☐

SHIRT ☐ SHORTS ☐ SOCKS ☐

NICKNAME KNOWLEDGE

EVERY CLUB HAS AT LEAST ONE NICKNAME WHICH GIVES THEM THEIR OWN UNIQUE IDENTITY. BUT HAVE YOU EVER WONDERED WHERE TEAMS GET THEM FROM? TO HELP YOU, SHOOT HAS CARRIED OUT AN INVESTIGATION TO TRY AND SHED SOME LIGHT ON WHERE SOME CLUBS PICK UP THEIR NICKNAMES.

RED DEVILS

Manchester United adopted this name from Salford Rugby Club in the 1960s when they were training at their ground.

GUNNERS

Workers at Woolwich Arsenal Armament Factory decided to form a football club in 1886 and, despite a number of name changes, their original connection with the armament industry remained with them.

POTTERS

This simply is linked to the large pottery industry which exists in North Staffordshire.

SAINTS

The name occurs because the club was founded in 1885 by the young men of St Mary's Church, the mother church of Southampton, and in the early years they were known as Southampton St Mary's.

TOFFEES

The famous nickname came after a local sweet shop known as 'Mother Noblett', located opposite Prince Rupert's Tower, which forms the majority of the Everton crest, which sold the Everton mint.

THE MATTRESS MAKERS

Although an odd one, Atletico Madrid's nickname is due to their red and white stripes being the same colours as old-fashioned mattresses.

HAMMERS

Two appear on the club's crest and the name originates from Thames Ironwork Football Club – a team from which West Ham evolved from.

OLD LADY

In the 1930s, Juve had an ageing squad so fans used the word "old", which in Latin means "youth", as a joke. The second part, "lady", is how they referred to their club.

YELLOW SUBMARINE

Villarreal use this name due to their iconic yellow home kit, and because they have a lower profile than Barcelona, Real Madrid and Valencia.

KASPER SCHMEICHEL
LEICESTER CITY

YOUR RATINGS

REFLEXES
/10

SHOT STOPPING
/10

COMMAND OF AREA
/10

DISTRIBUTION
/10

AGILITY
/10

OVERALL
/50

FACT FILE

POSITION: Goalkeeper
BIRTH DATE: November 5, 1986
BIRTH PLACE:
Copenhagen, Denmark
HEIGHT: 1.85m (6ft 1in)
INTERNATIONAL: Denmark

DID YOU KNOW?

Kasper is the son of retired Manchester United legend Peter Schmeichel, who is considered to be one of the Premier League's greatest goalkeepers.

THAT'S A FACT!

To avoid uprooting his family, Schmeichel travels 180 miles each day from his home in Cheshire to Leicester for training.

WHAT THEY SAY

"I judge him on how he is as an individual – full stop. It's inevitable there will be comparisons but he's dealing with the situation very well. I'm pleased for him that he's finally had a chance to play regularly in the Premier League."
Nigel Pearson, Ex-Leicester City manager.

"He has invented his own style of play. He is very capable of what he is doing and he should be credited for that. If he keeps working hard and keeps doing his stuff he will help Leicester win football matches which is what it is always about." *Peter Schmeichel, Kasper's dad.*

FACT FILE

POSITION: Goalkeeper
BIRTH DATE: April 19, 1987
BIRTH PLACE: Shrewsbury
HEIGHT: 1.96m (6ft 5in)
INTERNATIONAL: England

DID YOU KNOW?

Hart holds the record for winning the most Premier League Golden Gloves (four), awarded for keeping the most clean sheets in a season.

THAT'S A FACT!

Hart became only the sixth England goalkeeper to reach the 50-cap milestone against Italy in March 2015.

WHAT THEY SAY

"Joe is the number one goalkeeper in England and I think he has improved a lot this season. He is only 28 years old and he must improve in a lot of things, but he is working hard to do it." *Manuel Pellegrini, Manchester City manager.*

"He was phenomenal. He saved everything. We had a lot of clear chances but the keeper had a brilliant game. We have to congratulate him because he's a fantastic goalkeeper."
Lionel Messi, Barcelona forward.

YOUR RATINGS

REFLEXES
/10

SHOT STOPPING
/10

COMMAND OF AREA
/10

DISTRIBUTION
/10

AGILITY
/10

OVERALL
/50

YOU'RE THE MANAGER

THINK YOU'D MAKE A GREAT MANAGER? WELL HERE YOU GET THE CHANCE TO PICK YOUR DREAM TEAM. USING THE PLAYERS AND FORMATIONS, SELECT A SQUAD NO OTHER COULD COMPETE WITH.

4-4-2

PROS: TWO STRIKERS MEANS AN EXTRA TARGET FOR THE FORWARDS.

CONS: MIDFIELD CAN GET STRETCHED & OVERRUN.

3-5-2

PROS: SOLID THROUGH THE MIDDLE OF THE PITCH.

CONS: BIG RELIANCE ON THE FULL-BACKS TO DEFEND & ATTACK.

4-5-1

PROS: SOLID! A VERY HARD SYSTEM TO BREAK DOWN.

CONS: THE LOAN STRIKER CAN BECOME ISOLATED.

3-4-3

PROS: PLENTY OF BODIES FORWARD TO HIT TEAMS ON THE BREAK.

CONS: CAN GET HIT ON THE COUNTER-ATTACK IN WIDE AREAS.

Starting line-up

Formation: 3-5-2

1. Neuer
2. Ramos
3. Hummels
4. Kompany
5. Pogba
6. Rakitic
7. Ronaldo
8. Hazard
9. Suarez
10. Messi
11. Aguero

Subs:

12. Alba
13. De Gea
14. Ibra
15. Ramsey

GIANLUIGI BUFFON

DAVID DE GEA

GK
GOALKEEPER

HUGO LLORIS

MANUEL NEUER

DF
DEFENDER

DAVID LUIZ

SERGIO RAMOS

LAURENT KOSCIELNY

JOHN TERRY

MATS HUMMELS

VINCENT KOMPANY

JORDI ALBA

MARCELO

FB
FULL-BACK

PAUL POGBA

IVAN RAKITIC

MF
MIDFIELDER

AARON RAMSEY

CESAR AZPILICUETA

NATHANIEL CLYNE

CESC FABREGAS

BASTIAN SCHWEINSTEIGER

TONI KROOS

EDEN HAZARD

CRISTIANO RONALDO

FW
FORWARD
(WINGER)

LUIS SUAREZ

KARIM BENZEMA

ZLATAN IBRAHIMOVIC

LIONEL MESSI

RAHEEM STERLING

ST
STRIKER

WAYNE ROONEY

SERGIO AGUERO

DIEGO COSTA

PICK YOUR SPOT

THE BALL SEEMS TO HAVE GONE MISSING ON ITS WAY INTO THE GOAL. CIRCLE WHERE YOU THINK IT IS ON THE GRIDS.

CHECK YOUR ANSWERS ON PAGE 61

SPOT THE DIFFERENCE

THESE TWO IMAGES OF THE ARSENAL TEAM MAY LOOK THE SAME, BUT THERE ARE 10 DIFFERENCES. CAN YOU FIND ALL OF THEM?

CHECK YOUR ANSWERS ON PAGE 61

DYNAMIC DRIBBLERS

EVERY FAN LOVES TO WATCH PLAYERS WITH EXPLOSIVE SPEED. BUT IT'S EASIER TO MOVE QUICKLY WITHOUT POSSESSION, SO WHO ARE THE WORLD'S 10 FASTEST STARS WITH THE BALL AT THEIR FEET?

10 SERGIO RAMOS

POSITION: DEFENDER
COUNTRY: SPAIN
SPEED: 19.01 MPH

9 FRANCK RIBERY

POSITION: WINGER
COUNTRY: FRANCE
SPEED: 19.08 MPH

8 WAYNE ROONEY

POSITION: STRIKER
COUNTRY: ENGLAND
SPEED: 19.37 MPH

7 LIONEL MESSI

POSITION: FORWARD
COUNTRY: ARGENTINA
SPEED: 20.19 MPH

6 THEO WALCOTT

POSITION: FORWARD
COUNTRY: ENGLAND
SPEED: 20.32 MPH

5 CRISTIANO RONALDO

POSITION: FORWARD
COUNTRY: PORTUGAL
SPEED: 20.88 MPH

4 AARON LENNON

POSITION: WINGER
COUNTRY: ENGLAND
SPEED: 21.00 MPH

1 GARETH BALE

POSITION: FORWARD
COUNTRY: WALES

SPEED:

22.93 MPH

3 ANTONIO VALENCIA

POSITION: WINGER/
FULL-BACK
COUNTRY: ECUADOR
SPEED: 21.81 MPH

2 JURGEN DAMM

POSITION: WINGER
COUNTRY: MEXICO
SPEED: 21.89 MPH

NOW TELL US WHO'S
THE FASTEST PLAYER
YOU'VE SEEN?

..........Dylan o'omell

STUDY CARRIED OUT IN 2015 BY CF PACHUCA AND ENDORSED BY FIFA.

1.

CAMP NOU

WHERE: BARCELONA, SPAIN
TEAM: BARCELONA
CAPACITY: 99,354
OPENED: 1957

SUPER STADIUMS

2.

WEMBLEY

WHERE: LONDON
TEAM: ENGLAND
CAPACITY: 90,000
OPENED: 2007

3.

SANTIAGO BERNABEU

WHERE: MADRID, SPAIN
TEAM: REAL MADRID
CAPACITY: 85,454
OPENED: 1947

4.

STADE DE FRANCE

WHERE: PARIS, FRANCE
TEAM: FRANCE
CAPACITY: 81,338
OPENED: 1998

5.

SIGNAL IDUNA PARK
(WESTFALENSTADION)

WHERE: DORTMUND, GERMANY
TEAM: BORUSSIA DORTMUND
CAPACITY: 80,720
OPENED: 1974

FOOTBALL GROUNDS ARE THE PLACES WE GO TO WATCH THE BEAUTIFUL GAME. THERE ARE SOME AMAZING AND HISTORIC VENUES SUCH AS THE SAN SIRO IN MILAN, REAL MADRID'S SANTIAGO BERNABEU AND OF COURSE LONDON'S WEMBLEY STADIUM. BUT WHEN IT COMES TO SIZE, WHICH ARE THE BIGGEST STADIUMS IN EUROPE?

6.

SAN SIRO
WHERE: MILAN, ITALY
TEAMS: AC MILAN, INTER MILAN
CAPACITY: 80,018
OPENED: 1926

7.

LUZHNIKI STADIUM
WHERE: MOSCOW, RUSSIA
TEAMS: SPARTAK MOSCOW, CSKA MOSCOW
CAPACITY: 78,360
OPENED: 1956

8.

OLD TRAFFORD
WHERE: MANCHESTER
TEAM: MAN UNITED
CAPACITY: 76,100
OPENED: 1910

9.

ALLIANZ ARENA
WHERE: MUNICH, GERMANY
TEAMS: BAYERN MUNICH, 1860 MUNICH
CAPACITY: 75,000
OPENED: 2005

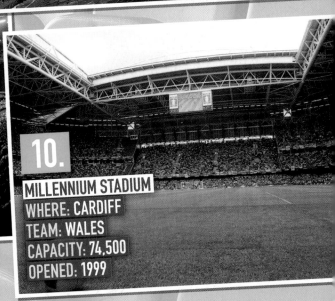

10.

MILLENNIUM STADIUM
WHERE: CARDIFF
TEAM: WALES
CAPACITY: 74,500
OPENED: 1999

11.

OLYMPIASTADION
WHERE: BERLIN, GERMANY
TEAM: HERTHA BERLIN
CAPACITY: 74,475
OPENED: 1936

12.

STADIO OLIMPICO
WHERE: ROME, ITALY
TEAM: AS ROMA, LAZIO
CAPACITY: 72,698
OPENED: 1937

Credit: West Ham United

WHAT'S IT LIKE TO BE A...
FOOTBALLER?

PEDRO OBIANG

POSITION: Midfielder

BIRTH DATE: March 27, 1992

BIRTH PLACE:
Alcala de Henares, Spain

HEIGHT: 1.85m (6ft 1in)

EVER WONDERED WHAT IT IS REALLY LIKE TO BE A PROFESSIONAL FOOTBALLER? WEST HAM UNITED'S SPANISH MIDFIELDER PEDRO OBIANG TELLS SHOOT EXACTLY HOW IT IS.

WHAT DO YOU LIKE TO DO ON YOUR DAYS OFF?

"Before I had a partner I liked to play on the PlayStation or meet up with friends. I don't play it much now but I'm still really good, I beat the majority of my mates. I also really enjoy watching films and reading, above all biographies of other sports people."

SO WHAT'S IT LIKE TO BE A FOOTBALLER?

"The dream of a boy is different. A child dreams of the stadium, the fans, lots of people, nice cars and trophies. But later, when you grow up and you're really inside the skin of a footballer, it's a lifestyle and a way of being. Everything multiplies eight times more than what you really dreamed it would be when you were little."

HOW OFTEN DO YOU TRAIN?

"Physically it's six times a week. But I would say a footballer really trains all day, every day, because when you aren't training physically you're training mentally."

WHAT ARE YOU ALLOWED TO EAT DURING THE SEASON?

"It depends where you play. For example, in Italy they are very strict and always eat the same diet made up of pasta, chicken, vegetables and fruit. When I played in the Spanish national team there was a buffet where you could choose what you wanted, and in England it is also a varied diet."

IS THERE ANYTHING YOU MISS EATING?

"Not really as I always have a moment to be able to eat one of them. As a treat, if I have won a match and have a free day, I allow myself to eat what I want."

DO YOU WATCH HIGHLIGHTS OF YOURSELF?

"I used to like to see myself playing on TV, but I don't anymore. If I know I played well then I don't watch the game. I will only watch them now if I have the sensation that I haven't played as good as I would have liked. I try to understand the details of why, so that's when I will watch the highlights."

DO YOU PLAY AS YOURSELF ON FIFA?

"It's funny as when I was young and I wasn't there I had to create myself and make it perfect, but now I'm there I don't use me."

HOW GREAT IS IT TO TRAVEL THE WORLD AND PLAY FOOTBALL?

"Not long ago I was reading in a magazine that one of the most important things is to travel because it allows you to renew ideas and put order into your life. Seeing other borders allows you to learn from other situations. Playing football is obviously the best way as it allows you to do what you like doing. You also find new stadiums, teams and nice places which is always exciting."

WHAT'S IT LIKE TO BE RECOGNISED EVERYWHERE YOU GO?

"It depends where I am. In Genoa, I'm quite well known, but in the rest of Italy people don't recognise me that much. They ask if it's me, if it's not me, and I try to go unnoticed. Sometimes if there is a big group of children I get worried about being stopped but it's always nice. If someone asks me for an autograph it means somebody likes me as a player."

HOW GREAT IS IT TO PLAY FOR YOUR COUNTRY?

"It's a gift of happiness. It's like a big prize for all your hard work during the season. Playing for your country means representing everyone that believes in you, so it's really nice."

WHAT ADVICE WOULD YOU GIVE TO KIDS LOOKING TO PLAY PROFESSIONALLY?

"I would give a child the same advice as a coach would give their youth team. You should enjoy yourself and learn to win and lose. At the end of the day that is what will always happen."

WHAT'S IT LIKE TO PLAY IN FRONT OF AMAZING CROWDS IN MASSIVE STADIUMS?

"It's very emotional. The first few times are quite difficult because you're not used to it - there's a lot of noise and it's very difficult to get that out of your head. But little by little, with time, you start to enter into a higher level of concentration. You start to succeed in turning off the lights and sounds and concentrating only on the game."

WHAT'S THE BEST PART OF BEING A FOOTBALLER?

"Sincerely... it's just playing football."

WHAT'S THE HARDEST PART OF BEING A FOOTBALLER?

"The difficult part is making time for your friends and family."

SUM UP WHAT IT'S LIKE TO BE A FOOTBALLER IN THREE WORDS......?

"It is perfect!"

RYAN BERTRAND
SOUTHAMPTON

YOUR RATINGS

SPEED
8/10

STRENGTH
7/10

TACKLING
7/10

HEADING
6/10

PASSING
8/10

OVERALL
35/50

FACT FILE

POSITION: Left-Back
BIRTH DATE: August 5, 1989
BIRTH PLACE: London
HEIGHT: 1.79m (5ft 10in)
INTERNATIONAL: England

DID YOU KNOW?

Bertrand represented Team GB at the 2012 London Olympic Games.

THAT'S A FACT!

As a 22-year-old, Bertrand won the Champions League with Chelsea when he made his European debut in the final against Bayern Munich.

WHAT THEY SAY

"I like him as a player because he's an offensive left full-back. He has shown his qualities from the first day but I expected this kind of quality. All he needed was to play every weekend and now he's doing that it makes him stronger and more confident."
Ronald Koeman, Southampton boss.

"He's a player with a great pedigree. I think he's enjoying it here; we gave him a lot of confidence, a lot of self-belief. He's matured now, he's a little bit older and everything's getting together for him."
Jose Fonte, Southampton captain.

FACT FILE

POSITION: Centre-Back
BIRTH DATE: August 17, 1982
BIRTH PLACE: Manchester
HEIGHT: 1.83m (6ft)
INTERNATIONAL: England

DID YOU KNOW?

During his time with Sheffield United, Jagielka was forced to play in goal for 34 minutes when Blades keeper Paddy Kenny was injured in a match against Arsenal in 2006.

THAT'S A FACT!

Jagielka is of Polish descent and his middle name is Nikodem, which means 'Conqueror of the people'.

WHAT THEY SAY

"It's great news that Phil is extending his relationship with the Club. He has excelled as a leader and as a captain of our football club for the last two seasons."
Roberto Martinez, Everton boss.

"Everyone wants to be king but very few want to wear that crown. A leader has to be there in tough times and sometimes put the team on his back, which is what Jags did last year."
Tim Howard, Everton goalkeeper.

PHIL JAGIELKA
EVERTON

YOUR RATINGS

SPEED
5/10

STRENGTH
9/10

TACKLING
8/10

HEADING
9/10

PASSING
7/10

OVERALL
38/50

TRUE OR FALSE?

CAN YOU SORT THESE FOOTBALL FACTS... ...FROM THE FIBS?

1

England international Raheem Sterling was born in Jamaica.

TRUE ☐ FALSE ☐

2

Preston North End's play-off victory in May 2015 was their first in 10 attempts.

TRUE ☐ FALSE ☐

3

Arsenal and Germany star Mesut Ozil is right-footed.

TRUE ☐ FALSE ☒

4

Manchester City have the biggest stadium in the Premier League.

TRUE ☐ FALSE ☒

5

Cristiano Ronaldo won the European Golden Shoe in 2015.

TRUE ☑ FALSE ☐

6

Manchester United signed Memphis Depay from Ajax.

TRUE ☐ FALSE ☒

7

No English manager has won the Premier League.

TRUE ✓ FALSE ☐

8

Zlatan Ibrahimovic has won league titles in Holland, Italy, Spain and France.

TRUE ✓ FALSE ☐

9

Germany beat Brazil in the final of the 2014 World Cup.

TRUE ☐ FALSE ✗

10

Chelsea play their home matches at Stamford Cottage.

TRUE ☐ FALSE ✗

11

AFC Bournemouth

Bournemouth are currently playing in the top division for the first time in their history.

TRUE ☐ FALSE ☐

12

Costel Pantilimon is the tallest player in the Premier League at 6ft 8in.

TRUE ✓ FALSE ☐

13

Bayern Munich have won the Champions League the most times since it began in 1992–93.

TRUE ☐ FALSE ☐

14

Philippe Coutinho is older than Ross Barkley?

TRUE ✓ FALSE ☐

15

Diego Costa plays international football for Portugal?

TRUE ☐ FALSE ✗

CHECK YOUR ANSWERS ON PAGE 61

ALL THE WINNERS!

PREMIER LEAGUE WINNERS

CHELSEA

WHO WON WHAT IN 2014-15?

PREMIER LEAGUE

RUNNERS-UP

MANCHESTER CITY

CHAMPIONS LEAGUE

ARSENAL
MANCHESTER UNITED

RELEGATED

HULL CITY

BURNLEY

QPR

TOP SCORER

SERGIO AGUERO
(MANCHESTER CITY)

26 GOALS

CHAMPIONSHIP

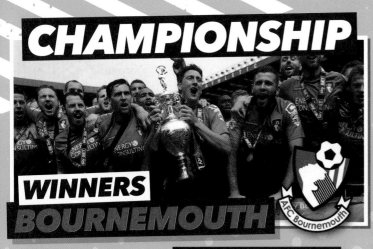

WINNERS BOURNEMOUTH

PROMOTED WATFORD

PLAY-OFF WINNERS NORWICH CITY

RELEGATED
MILLWALL
BLACKPOOL
WIGAN

TOP SCORER
DARYL MURPHY 27
(IPSWICH TOWN)

LEAGUE 1

WINNERS BRISTOL CITY

PROMOTED MK DONS

PLAY-OFF WINNERS PRESTON NORTH END

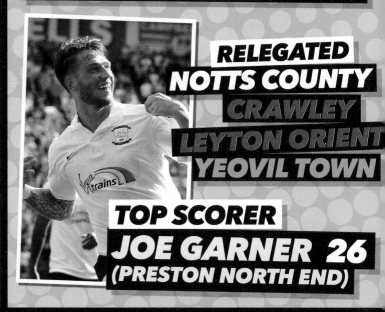

RELEGATED
NOTTS COUNTY
CRAWLEY
LEYTON ORIENT
YEOVIL TOWN

TOP SCORER
JOE GARNER 26
(PRESTON NORTH END)

LEAGUE 2

WINNERS BURTON ALBION

PROMOTED SHREWSBURY BURY

PLAY-OFF WINNERS SOUTHEND UNITED

RELEGATED
CHELTENHAM TOWN
TRANMERE ROVERS

TOP SCORER MATT TUBBS 21
(PORTSMOUTH)

CONFERENCE

WINNERS BARNET

PLAY-OFF WINNERS BRISTOL ROVERS

RELEGATED DARTFORD
ALFRETON TOWN
TELFORD UNITED
NUNEATON TOWN

TOP SCORER
JOHN AKINDE 31
(BARNET)

FA CUP ARSENAL

WINNERS 2015

RUNNERS-UP
ASTON VILLA

COMMUNITY SHIELD ARSENAL

RUNNERS-UP
MANCHESTER CITY

FA TROPHY
NORTH FERRIBY UNITED

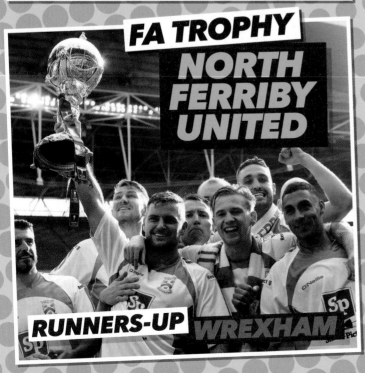

RUNNERS-UP
WREXHAM

LEAGUE CUP CHELSEA

RUNNERS-UP
TOTTENHAM HOTSPUR

JOHNSTONE'S PAINT TROPHY
BRISTOL CITY

2015 WINNERS

RUNNERS-UP WALSALL

FA VASE
NORTH SHIELDS

RUNNERS-UP
GLOSSOP NORTH END

SCOTLAND

PREMIERSHIP
WINNERS: CELTIC
RUNNERS-UP: ABERDEEN
RELEGATED: ST. MIRREN
TOP SCORER: ADAM ROONEY (ABERDEEN) 17

CHAMPIONSHIP
WINNERS: HEARTS
RELEGATED: COWDENBEATH
TOP SCORER: JASON CUMMINGS (HIBERNIAN) 18

LEAGUE 1
WINNERS: GREENOCK MORTON
RELEGATED: STIRLING ALBION
TOP SCORER: DECLAN MCMANUS (GREENOCK MORTON) 20

LEAGUE 2
WINNERS: ALBION ROVERS
TOP SCORER: PETER WEATHERSON (ANNAN ATHLETIC) 22

SCOTTISH CUP
WINNERS: INVERNESS CALEDONIAN THISTLE
RUNNERS-UP: FALKIRK

SCOTTISH LEAGUE CUP
WINNERS: CELTIC
RUNNERS-UP: DUNDEE UNITED

SCOTTISH CHALLENGE CUP
WINNERS: LIVINGSTON
RUNNERS-UP: ALLOA ATHLETIC

REST OF UK & IRELAND

WELSH PREMIER LEAGUE
WINNERS: THE NEW SAINTS
RUNNERS-UP: BALA TOWN
PLAY-OFF WINNER: NEWTOWN
RELEGATED: CEFN DRUIDS PRESTATYN TOWN
TOP SCORER: CHRIS VENABLES (ABERYSTWYTH TOWN) 25

WELSH CUP
WINNERS: THE NEW SAINTS
RUNNERS-UP: NEWTOWN

NIFL PREMIERSHIP
WINNERS: CRUSADERS
RUNNERS-UP: LINFIELD
RELEGATED: INSTITUTE
TOP SCORER: JOE GORMLEY (CLIFTONVILLE) 31

IRISH CUP
WINNERS: GLENTORAN
RUNNERS-UP: PORTADOWN

LEAGUE OF IRELAND
WINNERS: DUNDALK
RUNNERS-UP: CORK CITY
RELEGATED: UCD, ATHLONE TOWN
TOP SCORER: CHRISTY FAGAN (ST. PATRICK'S ATHLETIC) 20

FAI CUP (2014)
WINNERS: ST. PATRICK'S ATHLETIC
RUNNERS-UP: DERRY CITY

EUROPE

SPAIN
WINNERS: BARCELONA
RUNNERS-UP: REAL MADRID
TOP SCORER: CRISTIANO RONALDO
(REAL MADRID) 48

ITALY
WINNERS: JUVENTUS
RUNNERS-UP: AS ROMA
TOP SCORER: LUCA TONI (VERONA),
MAURO ICARDI (INTER MILAN) 22

HOLLAND
WINNERS: PSV EINDHOVEN
RUNNERS-UP: AJAX
TOP SCORER: MEMPHIS DEPAY
(PSV EINDHOVEN) 22

GERMANY
WINNERS: BAYERN MUNICH
RUNNERS-UP: WOLFSBURG
TOP SCORER: ALEXANDER MEIER
(EINTRACHT FRANKFURT) 19

FRANCE
WINNERS: PARIS SAINT-GERMAIN
RUNNERS-UP: LYON
TOP SCORER: ALEXANDRE LACAZETTE
(LYON) 28

PORTUGAL
WINNERS: BENFICA
RUNNERS-UP: FC PORTO
TOP SCORER: JACKSON MARTINEZ
(FC PORTO) 21

CHAMPIONS LEAGUE
WINNERS: BARCELONA
RUNNERS-UP: JUVENTUS

EUROPA LEAGUE
WINNERS: SEVILLA
RUNNERS-UP: DNIPRO

EUROPEAN SUPER CUP
WINNERS: REAL MADRID
RUNNERS-UP: SEVILLA

JORDAN HENDERSON
LIVERPOOL

FACT FILE

POSITION: Midfielder
BIRTH DATE: June 17, 1990
BIRTH PLACE: Sunderland
HEIGHT: 1.82m (6ft)
INTERNATIONAL: England

DID YOU KNOW?

Henderson nearly joined Fulham from Liverpool in 2012 as part of a deal for Clint Dempsey, but rejected the move.

THAT'S A FACT!

Henderson signed a new five-year contract at Liverpool in April 2015 that will keep him at the club until 2020.

WHAT THEY SAY

"Jordan showed through thick and thin that he is prepared to dig deep and go in where it hurts to turn these fans around. It sums him up first and foremost as a man but also as a player."
Steven Gerrard, ex-Liverpool and England team-mate.

"He is the type of lad as a manager you want in your team. He is never happy with what he is doing, he always wants to improve and, with the improvement we have seen in the last two years, he is now one of the top midfielders in the country."
Jamie Carragher, ex-Liverpool team-mate.

YOUR RATINGS

SPEED	7/10
STRENGTH	7/10
TACKLING	8/10
PASSING	9/10
SHOOTING	9/10
OVERALL	40/50

RYAN
MASON
TOTTENHAM HOTSPUR

FACT FILE

POSITION: Midfielder
BIRTH DATE: June 13, 1991
BIRTH PLACE: Enfield
HEIGHT: 1.78m (5ft 10in)
INTERNATIONAL: England

DID YOU KNOW?

Mason went from playing on loan at League One side Swindon to earning an England call-up in the space of just 13 months.

THAT'S A FACT!

The midfielder scored on his Spurs debut in a League Cup victory against Nottingham Forest.

WHAT THEY SAY

"When I was in the youth team, he was someone I always modelled myself on - an incredible player. It's been great to see him do so well in the games he's started, he has probably been one of our best players." *Harry Kane, Tottenham and England team-mate.*

"I always thought if someone put their trust in him they would have some player. The most important thing is when you get your chance, you take it. He's shown a lot of guts and determination. He deserves his breakthrough." *Micky Hazard, former Tottenham midfielder.*

YOUR RATINGS

SPEED
6/10

STRENGTH
7/10

TACKLING
7/10

PASSING
8/10

SHOOTING
7/10

OVERALL
35/50

SHOOT BUMP

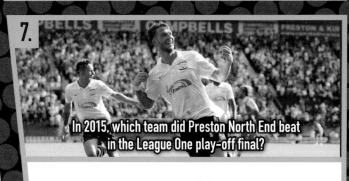

The voice of football

THINK YOU KNOW FOOTBALL? HERE'S YOUR CHANCE TO TEST YOUR KNOWLEDGE IN OUR BUMPER QUIZ. TRY AND ANSWER THESE 20 QUESTIONS. YOU GET ONE POINT FOR EACH CORRECT ANSWER.

1. Chelsea manager Jose Mourinho is from which country?

Portugal

2.  Who scored Barcelona's first goal in the 2015 Champions League final?

rakitic

3.  In which country do Dnipro play their football?

Ukraine

4.  Where do Stoke City play their home matches?

brittania

5. Which striker was the top scoring Englishman in the 2014–15 Premier League season?

Kane

6.  In 2015, which team did Norwich City beat in the Championship play-off final?

Middlesbrough

7.  In 2015, which team did Preston North End beat in the League One play-off final?

8. 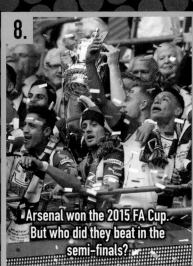 Arsenal won the 2015 FA Cup. But who did they beat in the semi-finals?

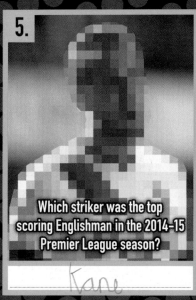

MPER QUIZ

9.
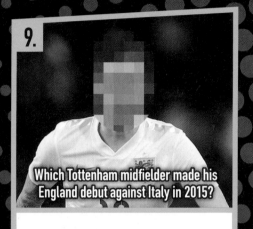
Which Tottenham midfielder made his England debut against Italy in 2015?

10.

Who did Dick Advocaat replace as Sunderland manager?

11.
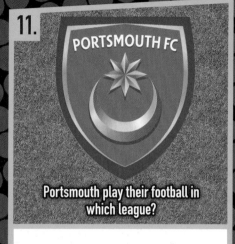
Portsmouth play their football in which league?

12.

How many Premier League titles have Man United won?

13.

What nationality is Southampton defender Maya Yoshida?

14.
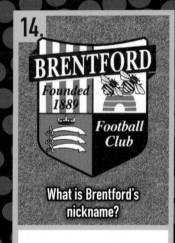
What is Brentford's nickname?

15.

Which club did Liverpool sign Mario Balotelli from?

16.
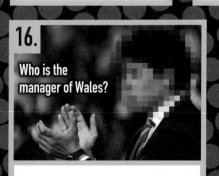
Who is the manager of Wales?

17.

Man City defender Dedryck Boyata joined which Scottish team in the summer of 2015 ?

18.

Who is England's all-time record appearance holder?

19.

Which League Two teams compete in the Devon derby?

20.

Steven Gerrard joined which MLS side in 2015?

The half-time whistle has blown. Grab a drink and head to page 52 for the 2nd half!

CONNECT FOUR

USE THE CLUES BELOW TO WORK OUT WHO THE FOUR PREMIER LEAGUE STARS ARE. GOOD LUCK!

CHECK YOUR ANSWERS ON PAGE 61

PREVIOUS CLUB	POSITION	NATIONALITY	CURRENT CLUB
1 — THE CELTIC FOOTBALL CLUB 1888	GK	ENGLISH	SOUTHAMPTON FC
2 — NEWCASTLE UNITED	DF	FRENCH	Arsenal
3 — FCB	MF	SPANISH	CHELSEA FOOTBALL CLUB
4 — BURNLEY FOOTBALL CLUB	FW	ENGLISH	LIVERPOOL FOOTBALL CLUB YOU'LL NEVER WALK ALONE EST.1892

PLAYER 1 ....

PLAYER 2 ....

PLAYER 3 ....

PLAYER 4 ....

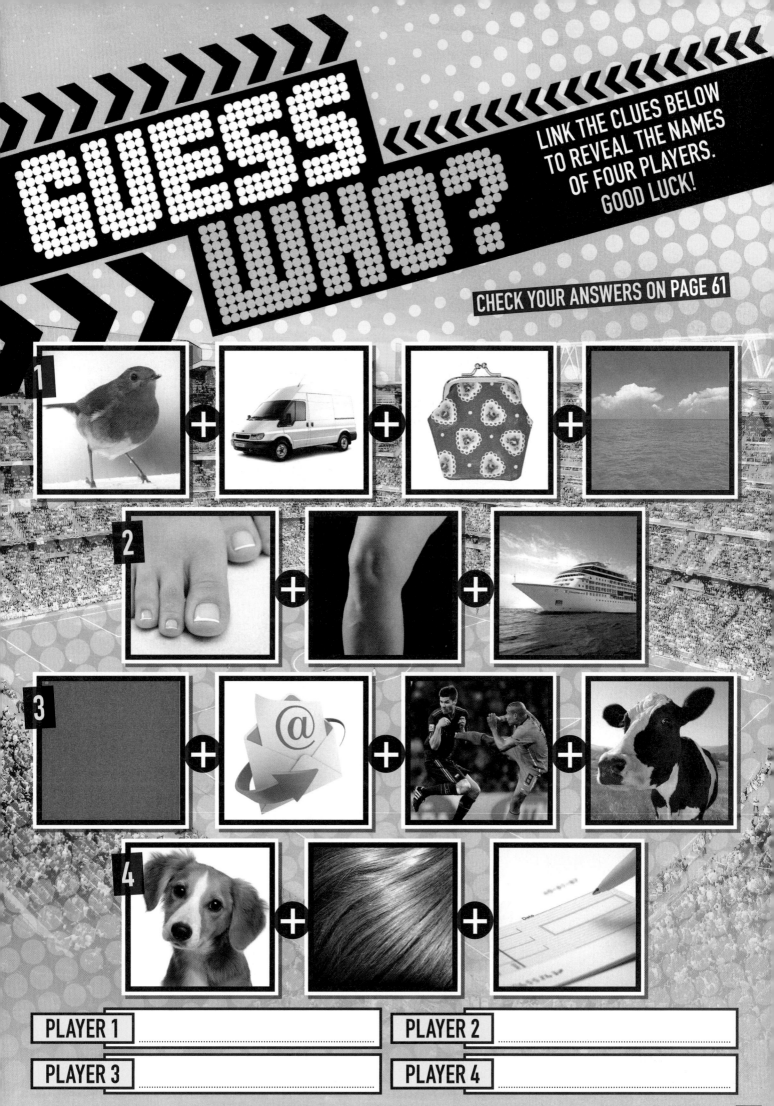

DID YOU KNOW?

THE INTEREST IN FOOTBALL MAKES IT HARD FOR PLAYERS AND MANAGERS TO HIDE ANYTHING FROM THE MEDIA. BUT HERE WE SHARE WITH YOU SOME SECRETS THAT YOU MAY NOT KNOW ABOUT THE FACES OF THE GAME.

Patrick Bamford turned down a place at the world famous Harvard University to pursue a career as a professional footballer.

Barcelona's 2014-15 treble winning manager Luis Enrique has taken part in four marathons and one Ironman triathlon.

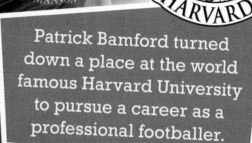

Croatia and Liverpool defender Dejan Lovren has his own clothing label named Russell Brown.

Manchester United forward Memphis Depay is a talented rapper and had to choose whether to play football or go into the music industry.

No way man! You are not faster than me!!

BINGOOOO OOOOOOO OOOOOOO OOOOO!

Hector Bellerin can run 40m in 4.42 seconds, quicker than Usain Bolt's split time over that distance of 4.64s when he broke the 100m world record.

Real Madrid and Portugal superstar Cristiano Ronaldo loves to play Bingo.

One of Chelsea captain John Terry's many pre-match superstitions is listening to the same Usher CD in the car before every game.

Despite having played around the world, there's nothing David Beckham likes more than visiting his favourite Pie & Mash shop in Waltham Abbey, Essex.

Argentina star Carlos Tevez loved eating Fish & Chips during his time in England.

Brazilian legend Ronaldo appeared as a guest star in an episode of The Simpsons.

Rio Ferdinand, Ryan Giggs, Gary Neville and Clarence Seedorf are just a few legendary footballers who own a restaurant.

SUPER STOPPERS

GOALKEEPER HASN'T ALWAYS BEEN THE MOST FASHIONABLE POSITION TO PLAY. BUT WITH THE CURRENT GENERATION OF WORLD-CLASS STOPPERS, WEARING THE NUMBER 1 SHIRT HAS SUDDENLY BECOME COOL AGAIN. HERE'S SHOOT'S TOP 10 SUPER STOPPERS.

DAVID DE GEA

D.O.B: 07.11.1990
HEIGHT: 1.92M (6FT 4IN)

NATIONALITY
SPANISH

The Madrid-born star showed amazing shot- stopping skills in the 2013-14 and 2014-15 season with Manchester United, resulting in him become Spain's new number 1.

MANUEL NEUER

D.O.B: 27.03.1986
HEIGHT: 1.93M (6FT 4IN)

NATIONALITY
GERMAN

By the age of 28, the 'sweeper-keeper' had won almost everything there is to win in the game, including the Champions League and World Cup. The German's style is very unique, but very effective.

GIANLUIGI BUFFON

D.O.B: 28.01.1978
HEIGHT: 1.91M (6FT 3IN)

NATIONALITY
ITALIAN

Despite being one of the veterans in the world of goalkeeping, Gianluigi Buffon is still as good as he's ever been. The Italian was signed for £32.6m in 2001, making him the world's most expensive stopper.

IKER CASILLAS

D.O.B: 20.05.1981
HEIGHT: 1.85M (6FT 1IN)

NATIONALITY
SPANISH

Despite a dip in form in recent years, Casillas is the most decorated goalkeeper to have ever played the game. He's literally won everything and made his debut for Real Madrid aged 18.

CLAUDIO **BRAVO**

D.O.B: 13.04.1983
HEIGHT: 1.84m (6FT 0IN)

NATIONALITY
CHILEAN

A brave goalkeeper with fantastic agility, the South American won the treble in his first season as Barcelona's number 1 in 2014-15. The Catalans forked out £9.7m for the Chile star.

PETR **CECH**

D.O.B: 20.05.1982
HEIGHT: 1.96m (6FT 5IN)

NATIONALITY
CZECH

Was a mainstay in the Chelsea side between 2004-2014, winning 13 major trophies. A calming presence for his defence, Cech is a master at commanding his area and making the goal look smaller for opposing strikers.

THIBAUT **COURTOIS**

D.O.B: 11.05.1992
HEIGHT: 1.99m (6FT 6IN)

NATIONALITY
BELGIAN

A giant of a man, the Belgian won La Liga, Premier League, Europa League and played at the World Cup by the age of just 23. The fact he replaced long-term Chelsea star Petr Cech shows how good he is.

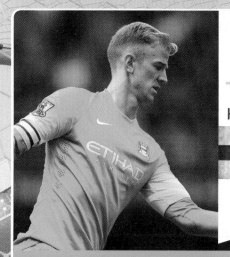

JOE **HART**

D.O.B: 19.04.1987
HEIGHT: 1.96m (6FT 5IN)

NATIONALITY
ENGLISH

After breaking into the England squad in 2010, Hart has held onto the number 1 shirt ever since. The charismatic stopper cost Manchester City just £1.5m and he's won the FA Cup, League Cup and two Premier League titles.

HUGO **LLORIS**

D.O.B: 26.12.1986
HEIGHT: 1.88m (6FT 2IN)

NATIONALITY
FRENCH

Known for his cat-like reflexes, Lloris has impressed wherever he's played. His performances and leadership from the back have seen him become captain for his country.

JAN **OBLAK**

D.O.B: 07.01.1993
HEIGHT: 1.86m (6FT 1IN)

NATIONALITY
SLOVENIAN

Despite still being young in goalkeeping terms, the Slovenian has already played for Benfica and Atletico Madrid – the latter of which paid £12.6m, making him the most expensive stopper in La Liga history at the time.

CELEBRITY

Here's a look at a selection of famous faces that have revealed to Shoot just how much they love to support their club.

OLLY MURS
TEAM: MAN UNITED

SIMON RIX & NICK BAINES
(KAISER CHIEFS)

TEAM: LEEDS UNITED

LETHAL BIZZLE
TEAM: ARSENAL

CARL FOGARTY
TEAM: BLACKBURN ROVERS

FRANKY FRYER
(SOCCER AM)

TEAM: TOTTENHAM HOTSPUR

DANNY JONES
(McBUSTED)

TEAM: BOLTON WANDERERS

SAM BAILEY
TEAM: LEICESTER CITY

TUBES
(SOCCER AM)

TEAM: CHESLEA

Want to read what the stars say about their clubs?
Visit **shoot.co.uk** for the latest celebrity fan interviews.

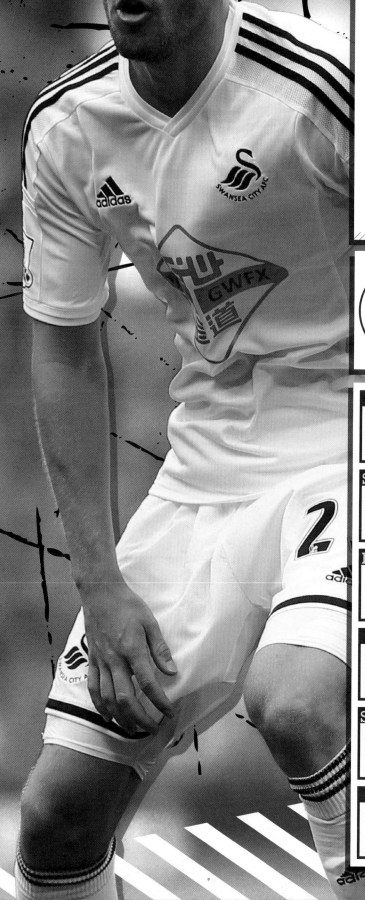

SIGURDSSON

SWANSEA CITY

FACT FILE

POSITION: Midfielder

BIRTH DATE: Sept 8, 1989

BIRTH PLACE:
Hafnarfjorour, Iceland

HEIGHT: 1.86m (6ft 1in)

INTERNATIONAL: Iceland

DID YOU KNOW?

Sigurdsson turned down a move to Liverpool in the summer of 2012, instead opting to join Tottenham Hotspur.

THAT'S A FACT!

The midfielder was named Icelandic Sportsperson of the Year in 2013.

WHAT THEY SAY

"When Gylfi plays with the one up front, the onus is on him to provide more of the attacking side of things like a second striker. Now he's more of a midfielder again, but he's still a threat, still very dangerous. He links very well, sets attacking play up really well and is showing how clever a player he is because he can adapt like that."
Garry Monk, Swansea boss.

"Gylfi has been absolutely brilliant. I've played with him before so I know how good he is and how well we play together."
Nathan Dyer, Swansea team-mate.

YOUR RATINGS

SPEED /10

STRENGTH /10

DRIBBLING /10

PASSING /10

SHOOTING /10

OVERALL /50

RICH LIST

RICHEST CLUBS

Some of the world's football clubs are worth staggering amounts of money. So who makes accountancy firm, Deloitte's, list of the planet's most valuable clubs?

1. REAL MADRID
(SPAIN - £549.5m)

2. MANCHESTER UNITED
(ENGLAND - £518m)

3. BAYERN MUNICH

(GERMANY - £487.5m)

7. CHELSEA
(ENGLAND - £387.9m)

4. BARCELONA
(SPAIN - £484.6m)

8. ARSENAL
(ENGLAND - £359.3m)

5. PARIS SAINT-GERMAIN
(FRANCE - £474.2m)

9. LIVERPOOL
(ENGLAND - £305.9m)

6. MANCHESTER CITY
(ENGLAND - £414.4m)

10. JUVENTUS
(ITALY - £279.4m)

TOP EARNERS

PLAYERS

The enormity of footballers' wages is the subject of much debate. But the players at the top clubs make football fans worldwide come back for more and have transformed the beautiful game into the box-office spectacle that it is today. Here are the elite stars who earn the most annually.

1. CRISTIANO RONALDO
(£48.85m)

2. LIONEL MESSI (£43.49m)

3. ZLATAN IBRAHIMOVIC
(£22.75m)

4. NEYMAR
(£18.74m)

5. RADAMEL FALCAO (£17.40m)

MANAGERS

While there is much debate over how much the players earn, some of the world's elite managers aren't too far behind with many now earning similar to, or higher amounts, than the individuals they coach. Here are the bosses who annually pocket the most.

1. JOSE MOURINHO
(£13.2m)

2. RAFA BENITEZ (£11.4m)

3. PEP GUARDIOLA
(£11.2m)

4. ARSENE WENGER (£8.3m)

5. LOUIS VAN GAAL
(£7.3m)

SUPER SELFIES

SOCIAL MEDIA HAS BECOME A HUGE PART OF THE BEAUTIFUL GAME WITH A NUMBER OF HIGH-PROFILE PLAYERS NOW HAVING INSTAGRAM AND TWITTER ACCOUNTS. THE 'SELFIE' CRAZE HAS ALLOWED PLAYERS TO TAKE FANS BEHIND THE SCENES, AS WELL AS SUPPORTERS BEING ABLE TO GET PHOTOS WITH THEIR FAVOURITE STARS.

HERE ARE SOME OF THE BEST SELFIES FROM THE LAST YEAR...

ADEBAYO AKINFENWA & MARIO BALOTELLI

The Beast & Super Mario Balotelli

@realakinfenwa

Following AFC Wimbledon's 2-1 defeat against Liverpool in the FA Cup, the League Two striker decided to get a photo with the Reds striker.

ALEX OXLADE-CHAMBERLAIN

@alexoxchamberlain

Following Arsenal's FA Cup final success against Aston Villa, 'The Ox' jetted away on holiday and made a new friend, posing for a photo holding a monkey.

CHELSEA

@cescf4bregas

The Blues celebrated their Premier League title win with a parade of the trophy, and midfielder Cesc Fabregas wasted no time in getting a group photo.

AARON RAMSEY & SANTI CAZORLA

Tom Jenkins/Observer

The duo played a big part in Arsenal's 4-0 FA Cup final win against Aston Villa, and the Wales international took a selfie with a photographer's camera.

HARRY KANE, RYAN MASON & DEANDRE YEDLIN

@harrykane

Tottenham jetted off for a post-season tour to Sydney, and the England international took a photo with his team-mates during their flight to Australia.

DANIEL STURRIDGE, RAHEEM STERLING, SIMON MIGNOLET & MARTIN SKRTEL

@danielsturridge

The Liverpool stars posed in front of fans at Anfield during the release of their new 2015-16 kit, with Mignolet tasked with holding the selfie stick.

DAVID LUIZ & THIAGO SILVA

@davidluiz_4

The Brazilian duo managed to track down two young mascots that looked like themselves, and posed in the same way as their young lookalike.

ANDER HERRERA, JUAN MATA, DAVID DE GEA & ANGEL DI MARIA

@anderherrera

The Red Devils travelled to their away match against Arsenal by train, and Herrera decided to snap a shot of his Spanish speaking team-mates.

LOUIS VAN GAAL

@gh30307

The Manchester United manager quickly showed that he is willing to interact with supporters as he posed for a photo with one at Old Trafford.

NEYMAR & LIONEL MESSI

@neymarjr

Neymar snapped a photo of him and Messi following their 5-1 win against Sevilla, in which Messi scored a hat-trick to become the Spanish league's all-time leading goalscorer.

JAMIE CARRAGHER, GARY NEVILLE & ED CHAMBERLIN

@carra23

Sky Sports' Monday Night Football trio decided to snap a photo of themselves and a couple of the backstage team following one of their shows.

NEYMAR

@neymarjr

Following their Champions League final win against Juventus, the Barcelona forward decided to snap a photo of himself with the ecstatic Barca fans.

MARCELO, FABIO COENTRAO, CRISTIANO RONALDO, SERGIO RAMOS & PEPE

@marcelotwelve

The Brazilian left-back decided to snap a photo with him and his Real Madrid team-mates during one of their training sessions.

MESUT OZIL & PER MERTESACKER

@stuart_photoafc

Amidst the celebrations during Arsenal's FA Cup trophy parade, the club's official photographer managed to grab a great selfie of him with two of the Wembley goalscorers.

DANIEL STURRIDGE & STEVEN GERRARD

@danielsturridge

During Gerrard's last season with Liverpool before a move to the MLS, Reds striker Daniel Sturridge posed for a pic with his skipper.

FRANCESCO TOTTI

Luciano Rossi/AP

The veteran Roma forward took his mobile phone out during a game, after scoring his second goal against rivals Lazio, and photographed himself!

SPOT THE STAR

THESE 10 SUPERSTARS LOVE FOOTBALL SO MUCH THAT THEY'VE DECIDED TO GO AND WATCH A MATCH ON THEIR DAY OFF. CAN YOU SPOT THEM IN THE CROWD?

- PETER CROUCH
- MAROUANE FELLAINI
- DAVID SILVA
- ROMELU LUKAKU
- ANDROS TOWNSEND
- CHRISTIAN BENTEKE
- JONJO SHELVEY
- JAMES MILNER
- MESUT OZIL
- GRAZIANO PELLE

CHECK YOUR ANSWERS ON PAGE 61

HOW DID YOU GET ON IN THE 1ST HALF? WELL THE 2ND HALF IS YOUR CHANCE TO CARRY ON YOUR GOOD FORM OR MAKE UP FOR A SLOW START? YOU GET ONE POINT FOR EACH CORRECT ANSWER.

1.

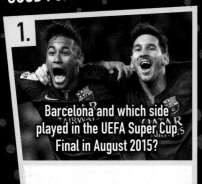

Barcelona and which side played in the UEFA Super Cup Final in August 2015?

2.

In which country do Fenerbahce play their football?

3.

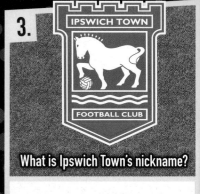

What is Ipswich Town's nickname?

4.

Where do Leicester City play their home games?

5.

Which Chelsea player won the PFA Players' Player of the Year Award in 2015?

6.

How many teams are promoted from the Championship to the Premier League each season?

8.

Which player captains both Swansea City and Wales?

7.

Arsenal, Manchester United, Chelsea, Manchester City and which other side have won the Premier League?

PER QUIZ 2ND HALF

9.
What nationality is Everton striker Romelu Lukaku?

10.
Barcelona and Spain star Gerard Pique used to play for which English club?

11.
Which country hosted the 2014 World Cup?

12.
Which two teams compete in the Tyne-Wear derby?

13.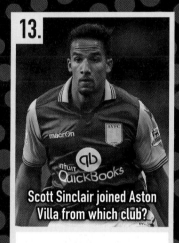
Scott Sinclair joined Aston Villa from which club?

14.
Frank Lampard is playing with which ex-Barcelona and Atletico Madrid striker at New York City?

15.
What nationality is Bayern Munich midfielder Xabi Alonso?

16.
Gareth Bale started his career at which Premier League club?

17.
Wigan Athletic play their football in which league?

18.
What number does Wayne Rooney wear for England?

19.
Name one of the two Football League teams that begin with the letter Y?

20.
Liverpool striker Danny Ings used to play for which other current Premier League club?

The final whistle has blown. Take a breather then check your answers on page 61 to see how well you did.

RONALDO

CLUB
REAL MADRID

DOB
05.02.1985

INTERNATIONAL
PORTUGAL

HEADING **10**

DETERMINATION **10**

STRENGTH **10**

FITNESS **10**

SHOOTING **10**

SKILL **10**

TACKLING **10**

SPEED **10**

DRIBBLING **10**

SET PIECES **10**

DID YOU KNOW?

By the end of the 2014-15 season, Ronaldo had scored 313 times in 300 games for Real Madrid.

WHAT THEY SAY...

"He has an extraordinary talent and he enjoys it with such a professionalism and seriousness that is difficult to find in a player of that level." Carlo Ancelotti, ex-Real boss.

TOTAL RATING

OUT OF 100

Vs MESSI

Ronaldo or Messi is a question that continues to split football fans. The Real Madrid and Barcelona superstars have been the two leading players on the planet for the past seven years, and arguably the two greatest of all-time. But which one do you think is best? Mark down your ratings for each and add them up to settle the argument as to who's better once and for all!

HEADING /10

POWER /10

DETERMINATION /10

FITNESS /10

DID YOU KNOW?

Messi has won the FIFA Ballon d'Or a record four times (2009, 2010, 2011, 2012).

SKILL /10

SET PIECES /10

TACKLING /10

WHAT THEY SAY...

"Cristiano Ronaldo has done a lot to deserve the Ballon d'Or, but for me the best player in the world, and already the best ever, is Messi, without a shadow of doubt." Xavi, ex-Barcelona team-mate.

DRIBBLING /10

SPEED /10

TOTAL RATING OUT OF 100

**CLUB
BARCELONA
DOB
24.06.1987
INTERNATIONAL
ARGENTINA**

SHOOTING /10

ALEXIS SANCHEZ
ARSENAL

FACT FILE

POSITION: Forward
BIRTH DATE: December 19, 1988
BIRTH PLACE: Tocopilla, Chile
HEIGHT: 1.69m (5ft 7in)
INTERNATIONAL: Chile

DID YOU KNOW?

Before his move to Arsenal, Sanchez scored both of Chile's goals in their 2–0 friendly win against England at Wembley in November 2013.

THAT'S A FACT!

Sanchez scored 25 goals in 52 appearances in all competitions for Arsenal in his debut season with the Gunners.

WHAT THEY SAY

"He's always wanting to go – he recovers so quickly mentally. We are not all equal in terms of that mental stamina. It's certainly exceptional to have such a straight impact on the team and on results in his first season."
Arsene Wenger, Arsenal manager.

"Sanchez produced a moment of sheer brilliance. The ball has moved all over the place and then off the bar. How are you supposed to get to that? He's a special player and that's what special players can do." *Shay Given, Stoke City goalkeeper.*

FACT FILE

POSITION: Striker
BIRTH DATE: October 24, 1985
BIRTH PLACE: Liverpool
HEIGHT: 1.76m (5ft 9in)
INTERNATIONAL: England

DID YOU KNOW?

The 2014-15 season was Rooney's first as United captain following the departure of the previous skipper, Nemanja Vidic.

THAT'S A FACT!

Three weeks after his 29th birthday, Rooney picked up his 100th cap for England against Slovenia in November 2014.

WHAT THEY SAY

"I like democratic leadership. He is always setting an example for the other players and maybe Wayne is the example for the team's fighting spirit. I think I made the right decision to make him our captain." *Louis van Gaal, Manchester United manager.*

"He has been a very, very reliable figure, and someone who embodies principles that we would all like to see — the England-born person and football player who regards playing for his country as something of vital importance." *Roy Hodgson, England manager.*

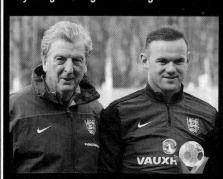

WAYNE ROONEY
MANCHESTER UNITED

YOUR RATINGS

SPEED /10
STRENGTH /10
DRIBBLING /10
SHOOTING /10
PASSING /10
OVERALL /50

FUNNY OLD GAME

"MY ICE-CREAM TASTES WEIRD!"

THAT'S BECAUSE IT'S A SKY SPORTS MICROPHONE THIERRY!

"CHECK OUT MY CRAZY MOVES"

MARIO BALOTELLI HOPES HIS BREAK DANCING SKILLS WILL MAKE UP FOR HIS LACK OF GOALS.

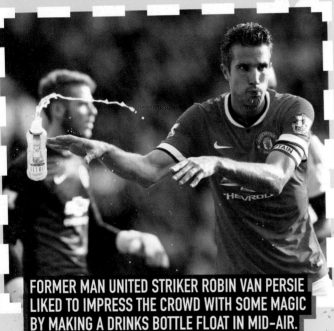

FORMER MAN UNITED STRIKER ROBIN VAN PERSIE LIKED TO IMPRESS THE CROWD WITH SOME MAGIC BY MAKING A DRINKS BOTTLE FLOAT IN MID-AIR.

"BBBBRRRRRRR!"

IT LOOKS LIKE CRISTIANO RONALDO FORGOT WHAT THE WEATHER WAS LIKE IN MANCHESTER.

"I WANTED AN XBOX, NOT A PLAYSTATION!!"

EVEN FOOTBALLERS GET UPSET WHEN THEY DON'T GET WHAT THEY WANT FOR THEIR BIRTHDAY!

CHELSEA'S DIEGO COSTA IS SO CONFIDENT OF HIS GOALSCORING ABILITY THAT HE HAS STARTED SHOOTING WITH HIS EYES CLOSED.

"WHICH IS LEFT AND WHICH IS RIGHT?"

CHELSEA CAPTAIN JOHN TERRY HAS FORGOTTEN HOW TO PUT ON A PAIR OF FOOTBALL BOOTS!

THIS ARSENAL FAN GOT TO THE STADIUM NICE AND EARLY TO SOAK UP THE FA CUP FINAL ATMOSPHERE. A DAY EARLY!

"HELLO! IS ANYBODY HERE?"

"THIS SELFIE IS GOING STRAIGHT TO SHOOT.CO.UK"

SAINTS BOSS RONALD KOEMAN WILL SOON REALISE THAT YOU CAN'T TAKE A SELFIE WITHOUT A CAMERA!

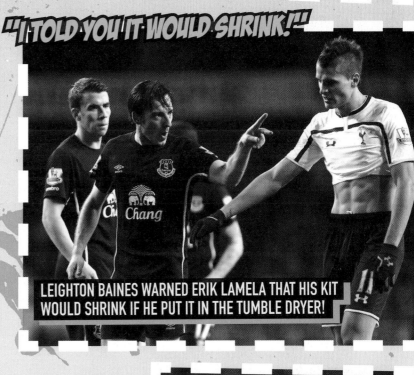

"I TOLD YOU IT WOULD SHRINK!"

LEIGHTON BAINES WARNED ERIK LAMELA THAT HIS KIT WOULD SHRINK IF HE PUT IT IN THE TUMBLE DRYER!

"YOUR BOOTS ARE SO COOL!"

"HERE, TAKE A CLOSER LOOK"

HARRY KANE HAS BEEN LOOKING FOR A NEW PAIR OF BOOTS FOR AGES, I THINK HE'S SEEN SOME HE LIKES!

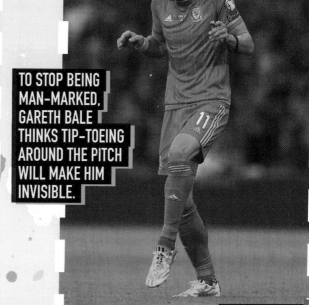

"SSSHHHHH!!"

TO STOP BEING MAN-MARKED, GARETH BALE THINKS TIP-TOEING AROUND THE PITCH WILL MAKE HIM INVISIBLE.

MY 2016 FOOTBALL CALENDAR

HERE'S YOUR GUIDE TO THE MAJOR EVENTS COMING UP OVER THE NEXT 12 MONTHS. IN THE SPACES PROVIDED WRITE DOWN MATCHES YOU'RE LOOKING FORWARD TO WATCHING, OR EVEN PLAYING IN.

JANUARY
Ballon d'Or Awards

FA Cup Third Round

FEBRUARY
League Cup Final

MARCH
Johnstone's Paint Trophy Final

APRIL
PFA Awards

MAY
Europa League Final

Champions League Final (men's and women's)

FA Cup final (men's and women's)

Football League Play-Offs

JUNE
Copa America

European Championship

JULY
European Championship

AUGUST
FA Community Shield

European Super Cup

Season Kicks Off

SEPTEMBER
World Cup 2018 Qualifiers

OCTOBER
WSL Cup

World Cup 2018 Qualifiers

NOVEMBER

DECEMBER
Club World Cup

ANSWERS

PAGE 08: Kit Swap
Gary Cahill: **Shirt C, Shorts B, Socks D**
Lionel Messi: **Shirt A, Shorts D, Socks B**
Mesut Ozil: **Shirt D, Shorts A, Socks C**
Diego Costa: **Shirt B, Shorts C, Socks A**

PAGE 14: Pick your spot
Game 1: **C4**   Game 2: **B7**

PAGE 15: Spot the difference

PAGES 24-25: True or False
1. True
2. True
3. False (He's left-footed)
4. False (Manchester United)
5. True
6. False (PSV Eindhoven)
7. True
8. True
9. False (They beat them in the semi-final)
10. False (Stamford Bridge)
11. True
12. True
13. False (Barcelona - 4 times)
14. True
15. False (Spain)

PAGES 34-35: Bumper Quiz 1st half
1. Portugal
2. Ivan Rakitic
3. Ukraine
4. Britannia Stadium
5. Harry Kane
6. Middlesbrough
7. Swindon
8. Reading
9. Ryan Mason
10. Gus Poyet
11. League Two
12. Thirteen
13. Japanese
14. The Bees
15. AC Milan
16. Chris Coleman
17. Celtic
18. Peter Shilton
19. Exeter City & Plymouth Argyle
20. LA Galaxy

PAGE 36: Connect Four
1. Fraser Forster
2. Mathieu Debuchy
3. Cesc Fabregas
4. Danny Ings

PAGE 37: Guess Who?
1. Robin van Persie
2. Toni Kroos
3. Radamel Falcao
4. Petr Cech

PAGES 50-51: Spot the Star

PAGES 52-53: Bumper Quiz 2nd half
1. Sevilla
2. Turkey
3. Tractor Boys
4. King Power Stadium
5. Eden Hazard
6. Three
7. Blackburn Rovers
8. Ashley Williams
9. Belgian
10. Manchester United
11. Brazil
12. Newcastle United & Sunderland
13. Manchester City
14. David Villa
15. Spanish
16. Southampton
17. League One
18. Number 10
19. York City or Yeovil Town
20. Bournemouth

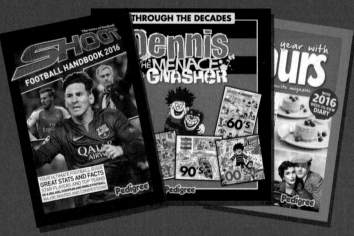